MW01617203

GRACE AND TRUTH

A Scriptural Response to an Unbalanced Philosophy of Christianity

"And the Word was made flesh, and dwelt among us, (and we beheld his glory, the glory as of the only begotten of the Father,) full of grace and truth." John 1:14

"For the law was given by Moses, but grace and truth came by Jesus Christ." John 1:17

Brent Logan
B.A. Th.M.

Grace and Truth
Brent Logan
loganofva@aol.com
(843)737-3129

Copyright 2015 © by Brent Logan
Published by
Victory Baptist Press
4000 Avalon Blvd.
Milton, Florida 32583 United States of America

ISBN 978-1-940791-11-1

Cover design by Pastor Nathan Brown

All Scripture quotations are originally taken from the Authorized King James Bible. All subsequent translation into other non-English languages are attempted to be faithful to that text. Any deviation from the King James Bible is unintentional.

Preface

The Bible says, "the LORD is a God of knowledge, and by him actions are weighed" (I Sam. 2:3). Too many times the actions of men are tipped to one side (Dan. 5:27). The same could be said of a church, religion, or a movement. "A false balance is not good" (Prov. 20:23). Certainly, the Lord Jesus Christ was the perfect balance on the scales of God, and therefore, He gave ministers to the church in order to perfect the saints so that they would all be brought "unto a perfect man, unto the measure of the stature of the fulness of Christ" (Eph. 4:12–13) instead of staying unbalanced children that are "tossed to and fro" (Eph. 4:14) and never "grow up into him in all things" (Eph. 4:15). Completeness. Maturity. Christlikeness. This is the need of a generation that all too often is stuck on one side of the balances of God.

For centuries the Christian faith has gone through diverse challenges, schisms, and divisions that have all affected the followers of Jesus Christ. Usually, the trouble was swerving into an extreme lane of overemphasis instead of remaining in the midst of the truth. The first few centuries of Christianity battled with a heretical one-sided view of the person of Christ. Either our Lord's humanity was overemphasized in the denial of His divinity or His deity was trumpeted to the expense of His humanity. While the names of Arius, Apollinarius, and Nestorius have been long forgotten by all but bookworms or history buffs, their names represent a failure to bring together the essence of the God-man. Jesus was all God yet He was all man. By the miracle of the Incarnation, He was not one or the other. He was both. If church history were to be fast-forwarded to the end of the Middle Ages, to the Reformation, an observer would see the great split of Christianity between Arminianism and Calvinism. Both of these philosophies were one-sided ditches where the Bible-believing Christian should not find himself, although believers in those generations were expected to declare an allegiance to one or the other view. Neither was right. Saved people cannot lose their eternal life nor are people chosen to salvation in eternity past without their willful choice. It did not have to be one or the other, but it was thought to be. Coming closer to our generation, church history had a massive display of unevenness at the turn of the 20th century. In reaction to cold, dead, formalistic religion, multitudes flocked to an emotional or experience-based Christianity. The rise of the Charismatic movement was an unscriptural overemphasis of personal experiences, but it was also a screaming rebuke toward a hypocritical, fake Christianity that had no personal relationship with God.

What do all of these events have to do with the subject of this work? Our day sees a similar one-sided conundrum emerging. It concerns how the Christian life relates to both God and man. Christianity has always been about God's grace. That same Christianity has also always revealed its converting power through the deeds of the men it has changed. A false Christian religion is nothing more than the works of men. An overcorrection of that misunderstanding is to say that Christianity is only about grace. To be in either ditch is to do a disservice to the claims of the Bible upon the lives of those who have been truly born again. Christianity is about Jesus Christ. Jesus Christ is about Grace and Truth. One without the other is a failure of similar past historical problems in the body of Christ. They must remain together. Christianity is not the philosophy of Do to Live, but it is the reality of Live then Do. To totally divorce the Do that should come after the Live is just as perverse as divorcing Christ the Life from Christ the Righteous. The sun or the rain is a different entity than the growing grass and blossoming flower, but they

4

certainly produce those things. They cannot and should not be divorced. They do not stand alone. They exist together to bring about the purpose of the Creator. Even so, God's free salvation of grace has a purpose of production in the eyes of its Creator. He desires growth. He desires to see the effects of what He has wrought. As the church of the Lord Jesus Christ is weighed by God Almighty, may we be found in the even scale of the image of Christ. May God deliver us from one-sided Christianity. Either side.

To place us where we are supposed to be on God's scale of Grace and Truth, we will examine the testimony of Jesus Christ, the apostle Paul, and other Scriptural witnesses.

May the only wise God our Saviour bring glory to Himself and grant His blessing on you to be conformed completely to His image.

Contents

THE TESTIMONY OF THE LORD JESUS CHRIST

Jesus Christ brings grace and truth, but not one without the other (John 1:14, 17). Our Lord was a complex personality. He was not a man of only one character type. He was the perfectly balanced God-man that always pleased the Father. The four Gospels reveal His life, words, and character. In them we find that He was both harsh and gentle. He was gracious and judgmental. He was tender and forceful, kind and angry. If you do not see all of this in Him, then it is obvious that you either did not read all the record or did not pay attention closely to what was written concerning Him. He was the whole package of what God Almighty wants in a man and only He was completely able to live and be that life. However, His life is what is to be worked into the children of God. It is Christ in us, the Spirit of Christ in us, which makes us the good, pleasing children of God we should be to bring glory to the Lord. That Spirit of God is described oddly in the book of Revelation. Four times we read of "the seven Spirits of God" (Rev. 1:4, 3:1, 4:5, 5:6). What is to be made of this? There is only one God and one Spirit of God. There is nothing mystical there, but I think there is a principle, which reveals to us the working of the Spirit of God in us as the children of God just as that Spirit was at work in the life of the Lord Jesus. The Spirit of God is more complex than one attitude or grace. He manifests Himself, if you please, in a seven-fold way to completely or fully express the character of God Almighty. The Lord Jesus Christ was the manifestation of this truth, having these "seven Spirits" (Rev. 3:1, 5:6, Is. 11:1–2, John 3:34). This multifaceted character of His is the same thing He seeks to develop in all believers.

Today we are deluged with one-faceted ministries, approaches, and philosophies. Do not misunderstand. There is one way to God, one way of salvation, one Bible, one Lord, one faith, one baptism, one Christian life, etc. However, this is the generation where so many have exchanged the complex life of all Jesus is for a simplistic one-sided view of Christianity. Let me explain. To fully be like Jesus Christ, you have to be more than truth. You must also be grace. To be like Jesus Christ you must be more than grace. You must also be truth. The delicately balanced Christian life, woven as a fabric in our hearts by the Holy Ghost, is to be a lifetime pursuit. Today we are plagued with a generation of professing Christians and churches that are emphasizing Grace Only to the exclusion of The Truth.

A properly balanced church or Christian would never emphasize only grace and liberty. On the contrariwise, neither should only godly works and restrictions be emphasized. The life of Jesus Christ is not all about lifestyles and standards, but it is not exclusively inward experiences and heart attitudes. Christianity is not all about fear, but it is also not all about love. The Bible promotes holiness as much as it does forgiveness. These things are not separate philosophies. They do not exclude one another. What we are to be does not ignore what we are to do. A one-sided philosophically anemic Christianity is not the fulness of the person of Jesus Christ. You can get in a ditch on either side of the road, but you will not find the Master there. He is multifaceted. He is complete. He is not nearsighted nor is He farsighted. He sees perfectly, and His vision is grace and truth.

It should be "the grace of God in truth" (Col. 1:6) that we are after for it is what is shown to us by our Master's example. It is grace in the shoes of truth. Grace that will bring forth fruit not only in you but also in all the world (Col. 1:6).

When Jesus Christ dealt with people while He was on earth, He did not just instruct them to love Him, meditate on Him, fellowship with Him, and stay with Him. Over and over, He told them to DO something. The doing was not earning anything, but it was expected. Look at how many times Jesus instructed people to do something in the Gospels.

1.   The Maniac of Gadara (Mark 5:19) believed on Jesus and was gloriously converted by God's grace. The man then asked Jesus if he could just stay with Jesus from then on. Jesus said no. He told him to DO something instead (Mark 5:19–20). Was doing something for Christ more important than being with Christ? Why did Jesus tell the man this? Was it not because He wanted truth to flow out of his life and mouth so that others would know the wellspring of real Grace and Truth?

2.   The rich young ruler (Luke 18:22–23) was not told just to receive and experience God's grace. Jesus did not tell him that the one thing he lacked was grace. Jesus told him to DO something. You may reason these words out dispensationally or spiritually, but you cannot change the words that came out of Jesus' mouth to this man. Jesus was trying to get truth into this man's life as well as grace.

3.   When Jesus was questioned about the manner of His disciples (Mt. 9:15, Mark 2:20, Luke 5:35), He said that when He departed they would DO something. Fasting is an effort on your part. Christ expected some deeds out of their lives when He left this world, and He did not leave His expectations to their imagination. He expected them to fast. There is not too much emphasis on these words of Christ for His followers. The truth of fasting for believers has been lost in the Grace-Only emphasis.

4.   While speaking with the woman at the well (John 4), Jesus did not tell her just to stay by His side and listen to His word and fellowship at His feet. He told her to go get her husband. Why was this important in the conversation? Why were the doings of her life an issue? Why not just tell her to believe on the Saviour and be done with it?

5.   When dealing with the lepers (Luke 17), Jesus did not tell them to stay with Him and enjoy His grace. He told them to DO something. He told them to go and show themselves to

the priest. One man correctly returned to worship and thank the Lord, but it did not change or lessen the command afterward. He was still expected to DO something in obedience to the Master.

6. Jesus said to deny yourself (Luke 9:23). Jesus said to take up a cross daily (Luke 9:23). Denying oneself is not enjoying oneself. Self-denial is rough. The Grace-Only pastor would never think to preach of the necessity of Christ's followers to say no to themselves about what they want or how they wish to live.

7. Jesus was a servant (read the entire book of Mark), and we are called to have His mind (Phil. 2:5, 7). You do not have the mind of Jesus Christ if you are not actively seeking to obediently be a servant to the Father and others. The last time I checked, serving was an activity.

8. At His ascension, Jesus did not say to them, "Ok guys, just rest in me, enjoy my grace, and everything else will work out great." No. He told them (Acts 1:8) to occupy themselves with DOING something (witnessing). How can the emphasis of the last commandment of Jesus Christ to His followers be a glorifying of man's works? His commandment, and its emphasis, is not a denial of the grace of God. It is the shodding of the grace of God in the shoes of the preparation of the gospel of peace to others. It is Grace and Truth. It is not just a good idea when the saved feel like it. It is a commandment of the Lord Jesus Christ for His followers to DO.

9. Jesus said, "do the first works" (Rev. 2:5). It was not just the heart that Jesus did not find right in the churches of Revelation. It was their works (Rev. 3:2 et al.). Grace-Only says that you just need to get back to your first love (Rev. 2:4). Jesus didn't preach that sermon. Jesus said to the church that they were guilty of leaving their first love so they needed to "REPENT AND DO THE FIRST WORKS". That is not a message of an inward grace but an outward expression. In other words, if you really loved me, then it would be seen in your

works. "This is love, that we walk after his commandments" (II John 6). If we love Jesus preeminently, then we will keep His commandments (John 14:15). Commandments are things we do. You can surely do the commandments and not love Jesus, but you cannot love Jesus and fail to DO what He expects. "For this is the love of God, that we keep his commandments: and his commandments are not grievous" (I John 5:3). If the expectations of Jesus Christ for your lifestyle grieve you or stress you out, then there is not a problem with the commandments; there is a problem with your heart. Loving believers earnestly want to please God. Lazy self-centered Christians disdain anyone who expects anything from their lives. First Love would erase these grievances.

10.   Jesus said to pray for labourers (Luke 10:2) not grace enjoyers. This is the Jesus of the Bible. He wants, desires, and prays for labourers. That word is pretty clear in the dictionary. It has to do with works. Jesus Himself did mighty works. And if we are to be like Him, then we will do the same works and more (John 14:12). This is not the deification of man, but it is recognition of Christ living His life through the believer. It is Grace and Truth.

11.   Here are more words of Jesus:

"For the Son of man is as a man taking a far journey, who left his house, and gave authority to his servants, and to every man his work, and commanded the porter to watch." (Mark 13:34)

This is Biblical Christianity.

12.   Jesus said if we are Abraham's children, then we should do his works (John 9:3). Faith makes the Christian a child of Abraham (Gal. 3:6, 7). Works makes no one a child of Abraham. However, according to the words of Jesus Christ, the children of Abraham will act like and do the works of their father. A study of Abraham would probably be a good study

on the example of Christianity. His life is filled with the grace of God upon a heathen man who dared to trust God and do what He told him to do. His life was Grace and Truth.

But, one might say, hasn't the world lost sight of the grace of God and replaced it with man-centered religion? No doubt. Surely there is too much emphasis on what we do instead of what Jesus is to do through us. The Christian life is not summed up or measured by what we have done. We are not right with God or spiritual or more pleasing to the Lord just because we give more, pray more, witness more, or give up more sin than others do. The Christian life is not only an outward form. It is to be an inward godliness with power. But you cannot ignore the outward. Jesus never did, nor did the apostles, or the written epistles to the church. Just because some get caught up in the unwise trap of comparing themselves among themselves, and putting men on pedestals, does not nullify the rest of the responsibilities that God places upon the saved. It must be grace and truth. It is the seven Spirits completely bringing us into the image of Jesus Christ.

What is grace? Grace has been defined as the unmerited favor of God, which is a necessity for salvation and Christian living. We can never earn or merit anything from God. But is this the absence of or de-emphasis of works?

Does emphasizing Jesus Christ mean that I am to ignore, not discuss, or preach about the works of men? If I am lifting up Christ, am I never speaking of man's works or his sin? If I promote the gospel, does this mean that I do not promote righteous Christian living? The Bible has the answer to these questions. My lifestyle, or "conversation" and "affairs", must "be as it becometh the gospel of Christ" (Phil. 1:27). God tells me that the way I live is important. A proper Christian lifestyle "becometh" the gospel of Christ, which is to say, our living should suit or make the gospel look good. Too many times just the opposite occurs, especially by those who believe that the way I live my life is an insignificant part of being gracefully like Jesus. Nothing could be further from grace and truth.

Do not misunderstand. Without the grace of God, all of humanity would be in hell. Salvation is not by any works of mankind. All my righteousness is as a filthy rag in the sight of God. No flesh will glory in the presence of God or boast of the acceptance of his feeble works. And yes, religion is the enemy of the grace of God. Religion says DO and you will LIVE. This is a heretical lie regardless of which religious system is doing the talking. Jesus Christ has DONE all the works. He is the One who is accepted. He is the Saviour that I must trust and cease from trusting my own works. Surely, if I sought to establish my own righteousness, I would be found in rebellion to THE righteousness of God in Christ Jesus (Rom. 10:3–4). Grace makes me accepted in the Beloved (Eph. 1:6). Hallelujah, Christ is in me by grace (Col. 1:27). And yet, that is not the end of the story. You are then warned and taught so that you may become perfect in Christ Jesus (Col. 1:28), so that Christ will not just be in you BUT "FORMED IN YOU" (Gal. 4:11). God the Father is seeking true representations of His Son in this world, and this will only be found when Grace and Truth are equally distributed in believers. Where is the manifestation of the full package of the character of Jesus Christ in this world? Where is that testimony? At the end of the day, grace is declared to be something you can see (Acts 11:23). Simply put, if you can't see the grace, then it isn't real. Anyone can counterfeit the grace of God just as surely as others counterfeit the righteous works of God. Genuineness weds the two together.

THE TESTIMONY OF THE APOSTLE PAUL

If any man had ever been acquainted with the depths of the grace of God, it was the apostle Paul. No other writer of Scripture speaks more about the grace of God than Paul. Even so, no other writer of Scripture speaks in such detail about the necessity of truthful living by those who are a part of the church of Jesus Christ.

Paul knew so much about the grace of God because of from where he came. He was not always Paul. He used to be Saul. As Saul, he made havock of the church of Jesus Christ. He persecuted Jesus and those He loved. His life was all about religion and nothing about grace. As a Pharisee and son of a Pharisee (Acts 23:6), he knew as much about the grace of God as a third grade student knows about astrophysics. However, you know the story. He met Jesus and was gloriously saved. He never got over God's grace and forgiveness concerning his past life. He declares that "the grace of our Lord was exceeding abundant" (I Tim. 1:14) to him regarding his past offences (I Tim. 1:13). This is why he thought of himself as the chief sinner (I Tim. 1:15). How amazing must the grace of God have been to him! No one ever deserved less from the Saviour yet was "this grace given" to he who was "less than the least of all saints" (Eph. 3:8). No wonder he writes more of the grace of God than anyone. So I guess this makes him somewhat of an authority of what the grace of God means in your life. I'm sure he would be a good teacher to us about the grace of God. That isn't all. Paul was divinely appointed by the Lord Jesus Christ to declare and define to the world "the gospel of the grace of God" (Acts 20:24). He was the caretaker of this mystery (Gal. 1, Eph. 3). Therefore, if I am a true adherent to the tenets of the gospel of the grace of God, then I must receive my instructions concerning this from Paul. For the Grace-Only movement this presents a most contradicting problem because Paul was definitely not a proponent of the philosophy of the Grace-Only movement. He followed the Lord Jesus Christ in emphasizing Grace and Truth. Let's examine his life and words.

The apostle Paul said by inspiration of the Holy Ghost,

> "By the grace of God I am what I am: and his grace which was bestowed upon me was not in vain [FOR NOTHING]; but I laboured more abundantly than they all: yet not I, but the grace of God which was with me." (I Cor. 15:10)

Do not tell me that the grace of God is ruling in your heart and mind if you are not abundantly labouring for the Master. You are kidding yourself. Paul is your example and pattern. Are you following it? Paul beseeched us "as workers together with him...that ye receive not the grace of God in vain" (II Cor. 6:1) and then lists a host of ways in how we go about "approving ourselves as the ministers of God" (II Cor. 6:4). Yes, God is supposed to get something out of me for the grace He has shown me. If not, grace came into my life in vain. We are to be workers together with Jesus. How strange that the modern ideas of grace include a false declaration that the grace of God is vain in your life if you are emphasizing some work or deed for Christ! This is the exact opposite of that very context in these Bible verses. The grace of God given to Paul was translated into building something for God (I Cor. 3:10) as a labourer together with God (I Cor. 3:9), not just enjoying Christ, but "in labours more abundant" (II Cor. 11:23) building something for His name sake. Jesus was not just in the house but also in the field and at the construction site. The gift of God's grace in Paul's life was to make him a minister to others (Eph. 3:7–8). If grace does not make you a minister in your daily life and work, then you have not been a good steward of the manifold grace of God that was given you (I Pet. 4:10). The real grace of God RECOMMENDS you to fulfil a work for God (Acts 14:26). Grace without works is a farce.

Paul, the great recipient and teacher of true grace, wrote to us the great doctrinal book of salvation without works in the book of Romans; but it is not a doctrine where works are de-emphasized after salvation. This same book says that "grace" is to "reign through righteousness" (Rom. 5:21). We only know grace is reigning in our life when God produces righteousness in us by His Spirit. Grace does not reign in wantonness or looseness. Grace reigns in righteousness. And if you think that the righteousness He is talking about is only God's righteousness and not yours, then you do not know the book of Romans. Romans 5:21 is the last verse in Romans 5. The context leads us into Romans 6, which is about how God develops righteous living in our lives through Jesus in us. I am not to let sin reign in my body to fulfil its lusts (Rom. 6:12). Grace does not nullify the power or presence or struggle with sin that I have while in the body (Rom. 6:1, 15). I am told to "yield" my "members as instruments of righteousness" (Rom. 6:13). This whole chapter is about believers living a holy life apart from sinfulness. This is how grace reigns. Don't tell me Jesus means everything to you when you will not yield to Him your body. Such is self-deception. Jesus on the throne of your heart is expressed through your mouth, hands, feet, and life. Furthermore, Paul speaks to us about the gifts of grace in the book of Romans. He declares that these gifts of grace are given to bring forth works and activity (Rom. 12:6; prophesying, ministering, teaching, exhortation, giving, ruleth) that we are to "do" and shew (Rom. 12:8). The rest of Romans chapter 12 also talks about things we are to do (be kind, not slothful, serving, rejoicing, continuing in prayer, distributing, being hospitable to others). This is more than just an inward grace of being. Grace is given so that Christ may do things through us as His body. His body is expected to be active.

One of the great Pauline epistles that mentions grace is the book of Galatians. Though Galatians is championed as the grace and liberty book for the modern anemic world of contemporary Christianity, it speaks of grace only seven times. The third time grace is mentioned, Paul says that God called him by His grace to reveal His Son so that he might preach him among the heathen (Gal. 1:15–16). There is your activity again. My friend, God's call of grace leads into Christian service. There is a greater purpose of God's grace in your life than your personal enjoyment. You are not so special to God that He just saved you to bless you and enjoy you. You are not that important. God is important. He called out a people for His name to show forth His praises (I Pet. 2:9). He made us new creatures in Christ Jesus to make us His ambassadors (II Cor. 5:17, 20). Christianity is not man-centered. It is God-centered. Centering something upon man does not just mean that man's works are glorified, but it can also be the glorification of just me without my works. In other words, many think that God's purpose for my life is just to enjoy me. I'm sorry to burst your bubble, but that is still just a different way to focus Christianity upon man. Focusing always on God's goodness and grace TO YOU as a philosophy is HUMANISM. God's purpose is not to be good to man but to glorify Himself and His Son. And the Lord is glorified when we let our light shine among men and become the salt in a corrupt society that knows not a holy God (Mt. 5:13–16). You may think you can bring glory to God by just enjoying God's grace, but that is not the testimony of Scripture. Our works bring glory to God when others behold them (I Pet. 2:12). Just because some do good works for self-glory doesn't mean that everyone is doing them for this motivation. Likewise, some people like to say that preachers are in the ministry for the money. Though I am sure some are, it just might be that such an accusation comes from the mouth of one who would be in it for that reason if they were preachers. The truth is that all preachers aren't in it for the money just like all striving in labour for Jesus aren't doing it for themselves. True lovers of Christ work earnestly that He may be glorified. It is the humanistic philosophy of a modern Christianity that must meet man's needs, satisfy man's emotions, and relieve one of personal responsibility so that I can finally enjoy MY Christianity and life instead of feeling burdened with all I must DO for God. All of that is still about you no matter how you package it with words saying it is all about God's grace.

Another epistle Paul wrote to teach us about grace is the book of Ephesians. In this great epistle we are told that we are saved by grace (Eph. 2:8–9). Man's works are filthy and abominable in the sight of God. Never, I say, never, before OR after the new birth can anything I do merit anything with God. When I pray, I am full of wrong motives and sin. When I witness, I often do not do so with a right heart. When I give, it can lead to pride within. When I sing, it can be self-glorifying and not with grace in my heart (Col. 3:16). Man's deeds are tainted with the flesh. This is undeniably true. But the next verse, Ephesians 2:10, is also true. After telling me the uselessness of my works, God Almighty tells me that I am "his workmanship, created in Christ Jesus unto good works, which God hath before ordained that we should walk in them". What an IRONY! The Lord says our works are unacceptable and then turns around and says that the whole purpose He changed our lives was to get us to walk in good works. Uncanny. You best get your head around that. This is the perfect balance of Jesus Christ. Your works are no good, but His works through you are expected. Every child of God has ordination papers. We are ordained and chosen for a life of good works pleasing to God. We cannot do these. We are powerless to perform. BUT He, oh my, the Creator, has created something in me that transcends my inabilities and sins. Christ in me can do the job. The Spirit of God in me can perform the deeds. He can make the prayers, giving, witness, labor, etc. profitable (Luke 17:10, John 6:63, I Cor. 12:7).

Ephesians 4:7 says, "unto every one us is given grace according to the measure of the gift of Christ". Why? So we would sit around and tell each other how wonderful His grace is all the time? Why? What do the rest of the verses say? Will you please read the word of God! You can't just keep lifting out verses from the Bible to support your philosophy without examining each of them in light of their contexts and with the rest of the body of truth. Jesus gave this grace into the lives of different people (vs. 7–8, 11) "for the perfecting of the saints, for the work of the ministry" (vs. 12). You have not been perfected if you are not involved in the WORK of the ministry. Does that make you feel uncomfortable? Does that burden you? Do you think that takes away from the exaltation of the person of Christ? It does not. The WORK of the ministry edifies the body and brings others into "the fulness of Christ" (vs. 13). This work that grace allows keeps God's people from childlike deception (vs. 14; say the 21st century) and grows them up (vs. 15) so that saved people will not walk like other Gentiles (vs. 17–32). Come on. Read the verses. Since when did the champions of grace, grace, grace, turn around and preach about how you should walk in your daily life? Doesn't grace just take care of all of that? Evidently not, according to the apostle Paul, or he would not have warned them about the sinful lifestyles in which they were engaged.

In Philippians, Paul declares that the same God that performs a work in you (Phil. 1:6) expects you to work out your own salvation with fear and trembling (Phil. 2:12–13). And to the Thessalonians he says, "Comfort your hearts, and stablish you in every good word and work" (II Thess. 2:17). The grace preacher never misses the truth of works in a good Christian life. He even warns us of the judgment seat of Christ by telling us that it will not just be about heart attitudes but about works (I Cor. 3:13–15, I Pet. 1:17, II Cor. 5). Therefore, "we labour, that, whether present or absent, we may be accepted of him" (II Cor. 5:9). He instructs us to always be abounding in the work of the Lord (I Cor. 15:58) and points to the examples of others who have addicted themselves to the ministry (I Cor. 16:15), telling us "to esteem them very highly in love for their work's sake" (I Thess. 5:13). We should emulate those who have worked greatly for Christ not those who say they just enjoy the grace of Christ.

When Paul writes of the grace of God manifested in the churches of Macedonia (II Cor. 8), he tells us they DID something. Nine times grace is mentioned in two chapters regarding them. They gave to "prove the sincerity" of their love (II Cor. 8:9). Is it not insane to say that grace is a mentality that has nothing to do with our deeds when the very opposite is presented in this whole chapter? Paul even defines grace in this chapter as an action (i.e. giving) when he says "this grace" and further defines it in the person of the Lord Jesus Christ in verse 9 showing us what Christ DID for us. We do not give to merit God's love (that is grace), but we give to prove the sincerity of our love for Him (that is works). You cannot have one without the other in real Christianity. And this does not just apply to giving, although the grace-movement churches love to include it to increase their need of finances. God makes grace abound toward us that we may have all we need to abound in good works for His glory (II Cor. 9:8).

Paul continues his explanation of God's grace in the book of Colossians. Though we have commented on several verses in Colossians already, one verse in this epistle stands out and says a mouthful on the subject of grace. "Let your speech be alway with grace, seasoned with salt, that ye may know how ye ought to answer every man" (Col. 4:6). Grace in your lips is never complete unless it is seasoned with salt. If you think that grace is the sole emphasis of Christianity then you do not know how to answer every man. It is grace with salt. It is grace and truth. Not just grace. Not just truth. Not just salt but not without it. If you leave out the salt in a recipe, then it is bland and unimpressive. Even so, God is not impressed when we refuse to couple the wonderful grace with the salty truth. Something becomes out of balance without this formula. The spirit is not right without the two together. The diet is lacking needed minerals. We must follow God's recipe. We should "walk worthy of the Lord unto all pleasing, being fruitful in every good work, and increasing in the knowledge of God;" (Col. 1:10).

THE TESTIMONY OF THE
PASTORAL EPISTLES

To say that preaching which deals with what man does or how he lives is misplaced or not approved of or desired by God is to reinvent Christianity, not only historically but Biblically. The belief that the pulpit should not address the way men live their lives in practice is an attempt to repudiate the greatest strides in the history of the church since its inception. Does the modern 21st century preacher really believe that he has found a better way than the men God used during the great advance of a Philadelphian age of preaching from 1600–1970? Were all of the great evangelists that turned millions to Christ really that deluded? Did Sunday, Moody, Sam Jones, Wesley, Ham, Bob Jones Sr., Norris, Whitefield, Finney, Booth, Spurgeon, Greene, Roloff, Jonathan Edwards, et. al. really not understand the grace of God? I know the reader can argue that the successes of men cannot automatically equate with the approval of God, and we shall address this later, BUT REALLY? Do you really think you know best now in this twisted generation? Are you smarter and more godly than almost 400 years of church history? Really? If you espouse that we need to stop preaching on the specifics of sin and quit preaching on man's responsibilities of service to God because it is not preaching the grace of God, then you must understand that you are passing judgment on the greatest movement of the Spirit of God in the history of the church since Pentecost. Are you really that confident that your grace-only preaching and grace-only philosophy is endorsed by Almighty God above all that were before you? Church history does not agree with you. The belief that we preach only about the grace of God in the heart and not about the works of a man's life is naive at best and arrogant at worst. I'm sorry. You are not that smart or that spiritual to redefine what preaching or church is supposed to be. The Libertines are in a battle to redefine the church, truth, and morality. What goes with that is a redefining of what preaching is. It is the spirit of the age and not the Spirit of God doing these things.

But of course, our rule is not the tradition of men, but it is the word of God. So let us allow the Spirit of God to define the type, words, and style of preaching from the final authority of written revelation. To this all people that believe the Bible should agree. Though Jesus Christ is the centrality of the word of God, each book of the Bible was given by God to us for a purpose. The Lord wants to complete our lives not just emphasize a part. Therefore, you have books in the Bible on wisdom, on prophecy, on the importance of Israel, on the life of Jesus, and on the doctrine of salvation, etc. The theme of each book conveys special meaning and understanding. There are books in the Bible that are written not to identify the doctrine of the church, but to instruct on how the church is to function and what the preaching and emphasis is expected to be in the church. Those books are I Timothy, II Timothy, and Titus. They have been called the Pastoral Epistles. If a man wanted to know the manner of preaching or the manner of the church, then he would be required to study these books intently. If he wanted to dissect the doctrine of salvation, then he would of course study the book of Romans. There are doctrinal books to show us what to believe, and there are practical books to show us how to present our beliefs. Paul wrote both types of books under the inspiration of God. In the three aforementioned books, Paul writes two young pastors to instruct them on how God expected things to go in the church. He gave them the pattern as to how they were to preach. Never has there been such a need to get back to these books as men seek to reinvent the church of the Lord Jesus Christ. So what did Paul tell these two men? Well, he begins by saying that

Timothy's doctrine should stay true and he shouldn't get caught up in controversial questions (I Tim. 1:3–4). Then, he instructs Timothy that he needs to see the end of what he is trying to accomplish through his ministry and the church. He tells him "the end of the commandment is charity out of a pure heart, and of a good conscience, and of faith unfeigned" (I Tim. 1:5). The end is that we want Christ preeminent in hearts. That is unquestionable. But how do we get there? We are not trying to get people to conform to a lifestyle without closeness to the Lord Jesus Christ. We are not trying to reform lives. We are not saying that Christianity is in what we do, but it is in a person. Amen to that. But how do we get people there? Do we get there through only preaching about the inward man? No. That is not what the Bible tells Timothy, and it will not work no matter what the intent. The end of the commandment is only the end. That means there is more to it, and there is a journey to get there. The writer of Galatians then recommends the LAW to Timothy (I Tim. 1:8). Did you get that? Paul's doctrine about the law was never intended to instruct preachers not to use it. It only must be used correctly. Paul goes on to say that the lawless, disobedient, ungodly, sinners, unholy, profane, murderers, whoremongers, defilers with mankind, and liars need the law preached to them. I think we still have those in our present-day. These individuals desperately need to see the law and not just grace. They need grace and truth. But was this intended to be a statement just for the unsaved? Even if it was, certainly there are unsaved people that are found quite often in church assemblies. They need to hear not only of grace but also the truth of the law. This is not what Grace-Only churches tell them. Furthermore, Paul tells Timothy and Titus that the believers need to hear preaching on their lives and works as well. As a matter of fact, much in these epistles is an instruction to these young men to purposefully preach on what the people in the church do, including the leaders of those churches. If this is not done, then you will have people wrecking their lives (I Tim. 1:19–20). Paul tells Timothy to preach to them that they need to pray (I Tim. 2:1–3, 8). The Grace-Only churches think it is misplaced to burden people or bring guilt in their lives for prayerlessness. Yet, the young preacher is to preach to them to involve themselves in the good work of prayer. Then, Paul the apostle tells Timothy he is to preach to the women in the church about the way they dress (I Tim. 1:9–10) and how they talk (I Tim. 1:10–12). Is this a modern day mean-spirited works-based mentality? No. It is Biblical instruction. It is the word of God! Paul did not tell Timothy just to emphasize grace in the congregation and the Lord will just take care of the details of how they live. That would be great, but it doesn't work and it is NOT the pattern of what God wants to be delivered in the church. Please get the doctrinal books and the practical church books straight! Just because you know Romans, Galatians, and Ephesians does NOT mean you are to ignore or fail to preach Timothy and Titus. As a matter of fact, the latter is the emphasis for the pastor to get the brethren to the end of the commandment. Paul goes on to give very strict rules of life and works for bishops and deacons. He talks about their "behaviour" (I Tim. 3:2), what they drink (I Tim. 3:3), and how their home life is (I Tim. 3:4). The same is true for the deacons and their wives. Now these are not things that Timothy should just know and believe. They are things he is to proclaim and teach to the church. He is to preach the word (II Tim. 4:2), and this is the word. He is not just to preach grace. He is not just to preach about the person of Jesus. He is not told that only matters of the inside are pulpit material. He must preach all these afore-mentioned things plus how men behave. This is called "all the counsel of God" (Acts 20:27). I know that is not popular. It is not desired. To the liberal or hidden rebellious heart, it does not sound very "spiritual" BUT it is commanded to be part of the diet of the church. And without it, the Timothys of the 21st century are being disobedient to their calling and the congregations have traded sound doctrine for pablum. We are not finished yet. We are just getting started in these books from God for the church. Paul is instructing Timothy on his sermon material so that all may know how they should "behave" in the house of God (I Tim. 3:15). Behaviour was important in the first century church; not just the heart motivation. Sincerity is no substitute for the perfect will of God. Chapter four of I Timothy is more discussion of the outward problems of believers, and these things were to be addressed by the man of God. Warnings against lying, compulsive vegetarianism, and the necessity to have a life of prayer and Bible reading (I Tim. 4:2–5) were things that Timothy is told to put the brethren in remembrance of (I Tim. 4:6). He is told to command and teach the church (I Tim. 4:11) about bodily exercise and a godly lifestyle (I Tim. 4:8). Are these just heart matters? First-century Christianity dealt with our example not only within but what is said, practiced, and read (I Tim. 4:12). We must not only take heed to doctrine but to ourselves (I Tim. 4:16). This includes everything about us, including the bodily works we do. The church of the Lord Jesus Christ emphasizes widows and the responsibilities of relatives (I Tim. 5:3–4, 8, 16). This is part of the Christian life! Paul goes so far to say that Timothy must look at a Christian widow's LIFESTYLE before supporting her (I Tim. 5:3, 5, 9, 10) and give a charge to widows and the church about this matter (I Tim. 5:7). If she doesn't pray enough (I Tim. 5:5) or lives in pleasure too much (I Tim. 5:6), then she doesn't make the cut. The entire church needs to know that she is to be judged by her testimony "for good works" (I Tim. 5:10). How's that for grace? Looks like he is dealing with believers' works doesn't it? That is what He says. He goes on. The younger widows should be preached to and scrutinized for support based on, not their close heart with Jesus, but by whether or not they are idle, tattlers, or busybodies (I Tim. 5:11). Good church-age pulpit speech includes all this plus the fact that these young women should marry, bear children, and guide the house (I Tim. 5:13). Not such a good topic for Sunday is it? Not in a church that is uninterested in historic Biblical Christianity. Good preaching includes how a church is to pay their pastor (I Tim. 5:17–18) and how elders are to be PUBLICLY REBUKED before the entire assembly when they sin (I Tim. 5:20). Now when's the last time you saw that? We are so far removed from Biblical Christianity that we can't even read the Bible and make personal application to ourselves. Don't you know that if you can't reprove and rebuke (I Tim. 4:2) people on Sunday for adultery, homosexuality, pride, laziness, stealing, gossip, drinking, nakedness, and cursing that YOU WOULD NEVER SINGLE OUT AN INDIVIDUAL for public rebuke regardless of who he is (I Tim. 5:21). Who are you kidding? I know, you want Christianity without rebuke and one where we close our eyes and pretend that we have no sinful lifestyles. That is Disneyland Christianity. I am telling you that these verses deal more with what God wanted preached and expounded upon by a pastor than any other books in the Bible. That is why I & II Timothy and Titus were written, to prepare the shepherd for the sheep. We have lost our way. I hope you notice that I am not trying to reason with you about my philosophy of the church, preaching, or the Christian life. I am just going through the verses! I can't swallow them so easily sometimes either, but I need it or it wouldn't be there for me. By the way, the purpose of the rebuke is not to harm but to help. This is not done through the spirit of arrogance but compassion so that these sins will be open beforehand to judgment and not follow the individual down the road (I Tim. 5:24). The last chapter of I Timothy speaks more of the outward ordeals of Christians regarding their "service" (I Tim. 6:1–2). Yes, Timothy is told to "teach and exhort" the people about their responsibility of "service" (I Tim. 6:2). AND, "If any man teach otherwise, and consent not to wholesome words" (I Tim. 6:3), which are found in this book he is writing, then that man, pastor, church member, generation is "PROUD, KNOWING NOTHING" (I Tim. 6:4). That's God's opinion and philosophy. What do you think about what He said? Timothy must preach about "men of corrupt minds" in the church (I Tim. 6:5) and materialism (I Tim. 6:6–10). This is NOT Grace-Only. This is Christianity in shoe leather, and it is the kind God Almighty is looking for or He wouldn't be writing these things for sermon material class. Timothy can't just try and get his church people to love Jesus and enjoy God's grace because he is too busy obeying Paul's command to "charge them" about how they are to look at and give their "riches" (I Tim. 6:17–18) and "that they DO GOOD, that they be rich in GOOD WORKS" (I Tim. 6:18). The REAL church preached that saved people needed to DO GOOD WORKS. If you can't see that right there in the Bible, then there is no hope for you. People do not see the truth in a King James Bible because they do not want to see it. Most people do not go to church today to hear a message about how they should do good works if they are saved. It is too invasive. So they heap to themselves a teacher (II Tim. 4:3) that will never be like Paul or Timothy. Just remember, although God never measures a man by what he does, He does expect something from his life. Let us move on.

Paul's second letter to the pastor contains a wonderful admonition. "Be strong in the grace that is in Christ Jesus" (II Tim. 2:1). What does that mean? Don't read a book about the Book to tell me what it means. The context of God's own words will tell you exactly what it means to be STRONG IN GRACE, and it has no appearance of the modern Grace-Only movement. To be strong in the grace of the Lord Jesus means to teach others to live a life of enduring hardness for Jesus Christ by not entangling oneself with the affairs of this life (II Tim. 2:2–4). It means to "strive for masteries" (II Tim. 2:5) and be "the husbandman that laboureth" (II Tim. 2:6). Is there no consideration or understanding to this meaning of grace (II Tim. 2:7)? Am I not a recipient of God's grace in order that I might have the power to "Study" and show myself "approved unto God, A WORKMAN" (II Tim. 2:15)? Am I not to emphasize in my life and the lives of others who name "the name of Christ" the necessity to "depart from iniquity" (II Tim. 2:19)? Does the grace of God nullify my responsibility or take away the emphasis of the possibility that I could be a dishonorable vessel to God if I do not purge myself from iniquity (II Tim. 2:20–22)? Is the Christian life of grace not about me being "a vessel unto honour, sanctified, and meet for the master's use, and prepared unto every good WORK" (II Tim. 2:21)? Is being saved not about me being "the servant of the Lord" (II Tim. 2:24)? Is there no message of repentance included with the message of grace (II Tim. 2:25)? Satan has laid a very nice trap for people today (II Tim. 2:26). We live in perilous times concerning what is inside of man and how he outwardly lives (II Tim. 3:1–9). Therefore, our beloved brother Paul emphasizes his "manner of life" (II Tim. 3:10) and godly living (II Tim. 3:12) instead of just grace living. It is the purpose of the word of God in my life to not only save me (II Tim. 3:15) but to furnish me "unto all good WORKS" (II Tim. 3:17). What does it mean to be strong in grace??? Does no one READ THE BIBLE??? The man told you. How can you understand being strong in grace in one verse without digesting the rest of the chapters around it from the word of God that tell you how? Quit rationalizing truth by defining the Christian life by your own experiences, and how you wish or think things should be. Submit yourself to the grace of God and what it is trying to accomplish in your life. It is the word that is to be preached (II Tim. 4:2) and not a philosophy of Grace-Only. Oh that God would grant us men that would "make full proof" of their ministries (II Tim. 4:5) by following the pattern of these epistles. And if by your faithfulness you find yourself alone (II Tim. 4:16) or with just one person (II Tim. 4:11) because you were obedient to your charge, rest in the fact that "the Lord" stands with you (II Tim. 4:17) while others forsake.

The book of Titus continues along the same lines as the epistles to Timothy. The pattern for the church does not change. What people need is the manifestation of the word of God through preaching (Titus 1:3) instead of a pulpiteer who picks and chooses Bible passages that fit his philosophy. Paul encourages Titus that he must "set in order the things that are wanting" (Titus 1:5). If he is to succeed as a pastor, then he must be found "Holding fast the faithful word...that he may be able by sound doctrine both to exhort and convince the gainsayers" (Titus 1:10). He must stop their mouths (Titus 1:11) and "rebuke them sharply" (Titus 1:13). What does this rebuke address? Is it the lack of grace in their lives? No, it is not. It addresses their evil character (Titus 1:12) and the fact that THEY DENY GOD IN THEIR WORKS (Titus 1:16). You can profess anything you want, but the proof is in the pudding. You can talk about grace all you want, but you have denied God if your works are disobedient or reprobate. First century Christianity had no time for profession, philosophy, nice lectures, and conversing together without good works to back it up. This is not the exaltation of man's ability. It is the recognition of God's work inside a man's heart that comes out of his mouth, hands, feet, and life.

A good, Christ-honoring church today will be constantly discussing how "aged men...aged women...young women... young men...servants" live their daily lives (Titus 2:2–10). You cannot get around it. This is "sound doctrine" (Titus 2:1). Sound doctrine is not defined here as the great truths of redemption, reconciliation, or the second coming BUT sanctification, as in how people live their lives. The greatest gift a church or community can have is a preacher that will preach about the way they live. The devil has stolen this man out of the church's pulpit and replaced him with a philosopher, theologian, or politician. Right doctrine shows "a pattern of good works" (Titus 2:7). Do not tell me of your doctrines of justification if "in doctrine" you do not show "uncorruptness, gravity, sincerity, sound speech" (Titus 2:7–8).

Now comes one of the most important verses in the Bible on GRACE. It is found in an epistle instructing the preacher and dealing with church polity. "For the grace of God that bringeth salvation hath appeared to all men" (Titus 2:11). The verse continues a believer's journey into grace and truth. This GRACE has been made known to all men. It is strange that many theologians who champion the Grace-Only movement are Calvinists. Calvinisim (i.e. not my responsibilities but God will do it all) is the logical end of the road of all of this Grace-Only philosophy and not just liberalism (aka the Libertines). The verse before us refutes this Calvinistic unbalanced theology. Praise God for His grace that brought salvation in my life. All glory to Jesus! It is all His finished work. That grace has made me accepted in the beloved. I would not, could not, be redeemed without it. But again, it is grace AND truth. Titus 2:11 is the grace. Titus 2:12 is the truth. It would be wise to balance that seesaw before you crash to the ground. Titus 2:12 tells me that grace is "Teaching us" something. Grace teaches me how to live. Grace teaches me "that denying ungodliness and worldly lusts, we should live soberly, righteously, and godly, in this present world" (Titus 2:12). Grace teaches me that this present world is my enemy. A real Grace-teacher will instruct a congregation about how they live in the present world. A real Grace-teacher will tell the flock about the dangers of ungodliness and lusts. A real Grace-teacher never just teaches about grace! You could say the same thing for the subject of the Holy Ghost. The Holy Ghost doesn't teach or emphasize Himself when He is in control (aka Charismatics). The Holy Ghost teaches others about Jesus Christ. Grace doesn't glorify grace any more than the Holy Ghost would glorify Himself. Grace teaches, according to the text of God's Holy word, about denying ungodliness and worldly lusts. Do you see that? Grace teaches not about grace but about how to live soberly, righteously, and godly in this present world. What a thing. Those who champion grace and speak always of grace are not even teaching the grace of God. That is not my opinion. If you major on grace, then you have your sermon material here. The real heart attitude of grace is the desire for purification, peculiarity, and being zealous of GOOD WORKS (Titus 2:14). Yes, that is what it says. Are you zealous of good works? No? You just want to emphasize God's grace in people's hearts? That is not why Jesus redeemed us "from all iniquity" (Titus 2:14). He redeemed us for a reason. He wants a pure people ZEALOUS OF GOOD WORKS. And if you are a pastor or preacher reading these words, then they have even more meaning for you. "These things speak, and exhort, and rebuke with all authority, Let no man despise thee" (II Tim. 2:15). Why would Paul warn Timothy that others would despise him? Because he emphasized unhindered grace, liberty, and fellowship with Jesus? Not on your life. He told Timothy to get ready for others to despise him for preaching against ungodliness, worldly lusts, while calling for purity in God's people, and good works in their lives. Now I'm sorry if that is not how you see it. I truly say that I wished that these words did not make you mad or ruin the way you look at Christianity. But this is just the Bible, my friend. It's true for you, and it is true for me. It was true 2000 years ago, and it is still true in the 21st century. If you love the Lord Jesus Christ, then you'll line up with it. Paul said in I Corinthians 14:37,

> "If any man think himself to be a prophet, or spiritual, let him acknowledge that the things that I write unto you are the commandments of the Lord."

Titus chapter three speaks much of grace. It speaks of the precious saving grace of God (Titus 3:5–7). We are "justified by his grace" (Titus 3:7). "Eternal life" could never be earned, but instead, graciously "shed on us abundantly through Jesus

Christ our Saviour" (Titus 3:6). Only HE can get glory because it is HE who accomplished "regeneration" (Titus 3:5). That is GRACE. But remember, grace is never alone. The next verse is TRUTH.

> "This is a faithful saying, and these things I will that thou affirm constantly, that they which have believed in God might be careful to maintain good works. These things are good and profitable unto men" (Titus 3:8).

If it is enough just to talk about the grace of God all the time or only speak of the person of Christ, then what is this? Immediately after the GRACE, Paul wants Titus to give them a dose of WORKS. And it was just not Titus who was commanded. Every man who holds the word of God in the church of the Lord Jesus Christ is commanded to "affirm constantly" the importance of believers maintaining good works. I just can't say it any plainer. God cannot say it any plainer. May the voices of fake Christianity be silenced by the word of God while we follow the precepts of being led in the path of righteousness for His name's sake. Not our name's sake. Not the glorification of man. Why is it that the Grace-Only philosophers think that good works can only be done for the glory of self? Is that the way they would do them? The truth is that good works can and should be done for the glory of God. It is heretical or subversive to reject these things (Titus 3:10–11). This verse was not an isolated thought as can be seen throughout the previous twelve chapters of the word of God. Neither is it the last thought in the book. Read further. "And let ours also learn to maintain good works for necessary uses, that they be not unfruitful" (Titus 3:14). Paul ends this book with a repetition for the church. A repetition of the TRUTH of GOOD WORKS, and then he closes with GRACE again (Titus 3:15).

You just cannot dismiss how it requires bonding together. It must always be grace AND truth.

OTHER SCRIPTURAL WITNESSES

We now look to various other books or passages in the Bible, which define grace and truth for us. Even though they have different authors, they will, of course, all agree with the rest of the words of God that we have already examined.

The testimony of the book of Acts is just that, it is the acts that the apostles did by the grace of God through the energy of the Holy Ghost. Thank God that the apostles were not Grace-Only proponents. They did not stay in Jerusalem to enjoy their Christianity but were the shakers and movers by the power of God. We would not be enjoying the grace of God in the western world without the diligence of a working Christianity on their part. The missionary movement is seen in full motion in Acts 13:2 when the Holy Ghost said, "Separate me Barnabas and Saul for the work whereunto I have called them." They were not separated for grace but for work. How wicked it is to put the children of God at ease in Zion while a great work of the gospel to the lost goes undone. As these men preached and led people to Christ, we hear them declare to the Gentiles to "repent and turn to God, and do works meet for repentance" (Acts 26:20). Does the church of the 21st century have a different message? It seems so since this is not the oft-heard declaration today. The works preached by these missionaries were not the means of acceptance by God, but they were MEET. In other words, they were fitting. They were right to do. Anyone who truly repents should be expected to do works that are fitting for a person who has repented. When there is no real repentance, there are no real works. Maybe this is also the reason that our generation has forgotten the doctrine of repentance in regard to salvation.

We also wish to bring in the book of Hebrews to testify in our discussion. We are told that "God *is* not unrighteous to forget your work and labour of love, which ye have shewed toward his name, in that ye have ministered to the saints, and do minister" (Heb. 6:10). The verse does not say that God will not forget your life that rested in His grace. Oh, no. There is nothing for God to remember from the life of one of His children who lazily did nothing with the truth of the grace of God in his or her life. This is why we are commanded to "consider one another to provoke unto love and to good works" (Heb. 10:24). To spur on your brothers and sisters in Christ to do more for Jesus is not a burdensome trait of a legalist, but it is the obedience of one who cares for the family of God, because God desires to make you "perfect in every good work to do his will, working in you that which is wellpleasing in his sight, through Jesus Christ; to whom *be* glory for ever and ever. Amen" (Heb. 13:21). God gets no glory from a do-nothing Christian resting in his liberty. His will is contrary to such a thing. Hebrews 12:28 tells us to "have grace", and then it tells us what that means. According to the verse, to have grace in our lives means that we "serve God acceptably with reverence and godly fear". This is an activity we perform and not just an inward experience with God. Here, grace is coupled with service and fear. Can you really have grace without this manifestation?

Adherents to grace-only theology usually shun the book of James. Even Martin Luther had trouble with reconciling the epistle with the truths of salvation by grace through faith. However, there is nothing wrong with James' epistle. There may be something wrong with me or with my understanding of the words God wrote through him, but James feeds our souls the words of God. In chapter 1, we are instructed to look "into the perfect law of liberty" and continue *therein* because the Lord does not want us to be "a forgetful hearer, but a doer of the work" so that we might "be blessed" in our deeds (James

1:25). The blessing of the Lord comes into the lives of believers when they not only hear the law of liberty, but when they are doers of the work through their deeds. So if the law of liberty is expounded properly, people are instructed to do something in their lives. If they are not engaged in these deeds, then either they heard the wrong message or forgot it. Then comes the great debate in the book of James. The following verses have been debated for hundreds of years:

> "What *doth it* profit, my brethren, though a man say he hath faith, and have not works? can faith save him?...Even so faith, if it hath not works, is dead, being alone...Yea, a man may say, Thou hast faith, and I have works: shew me thy faith without thy works, and I will shew thee my faith by my works... But wilt thou know, O vain man, that faith without works is dead? Was not Abraham our father justified by works, when he had offered Isaac his son upon the altar? Seest thou how faith wrought with his works, and by works was faith made perfect?...Ye see then how that by works a man is justified, and not by faith only. Likewise also was not Rahab the harlot justified by works, when she had received the messengers, and had sent *them* out another way? For as the body without the spirit is dead, so faith without works is dead also." (James 2:14, 17, 18, 20–22, 24–26)

However you choose to expound the verses above, you cannot disregard the proper place of works in the lives of those who have faith. At its simplest, you would come away with this truth. Just as grace manifests itself in truth, faith manifests itself in works.

"Who *is* a wise man and endued with knowledge among you? let him shew out of a good conversation his works with meekness of wisdom." (James 3:13)

Sadly, the book of Jude prophesied of these days before the coming Revelation of our Lord Jesus Christ. He said there would be those who would turn "the grace of our God into lasciviousness" (Jude 4). Notice, he did not say they would just espouse lasciviousness. No. They would take, hold, speak of the grace of God and then turn it into something else. This is not an activity of people outside of the church. This is a philosophy "crept in unawares" into the church. The spirit of the last days of the church before the Revelation is an inward cancer within the people of God. It is grace without boundaries. It is grace without truth. Grace without contending (Jude 3). Grace with lasciviousness (Jude 4). Grace without being put in remembrance of God's judgment even to the extent of His own people (Jude 5–7). Grace without contending with the devil (Jude 9). It is a feast of charity and grace in the church without any fear (Jude 12) and just a blustery day of grand cloudy activity but no real rain or real fruit. The last time (Jude 18) is a day of grace without shame (Jude 13) where there is no prophet like Enoch who will convince people of a fourfold judgment upon ungodly deeds (Jude 14–15). They just need to experience grace in the last days without worrying or hearing preaching about the deeds they are doing in their lives. This is a very nice setup for the removal of conviction of sin and repentance. Before Jesus comes again, people are sensual, which is the opposite of the Spirit (Jude 19). What are we to do? Nothing? Join them? Just emphasize grace and quit worrying about what we have to do? No. Jude says, build up yourselves. Pray. Keep yourselves in the love of God. Make a difference through your compassion to others and pull some out of this fire that has been lit. Hate, that's right, hate even the garment spotted by the flesh. Not just the flesh but also the garment in

42

which it is wrapped. This is the character of Jesus Christ. He loves righteousness and hates iniquity (Heb. 1:9). This is the appropriate emphasis. This is the contending we must involve ourselves in. And this is not for our glory (Jude 25)! This is not done so we can boast that we are more spiritual and godly than the wicked world. We do not contend to become accepted with God or merit His favor. But contrariwise, we do these things at His bidding. We engage in this battle to be obedient to our Master and Lord. It is His word to which we seek to conform ourselves. It is His glory alone we should seek. But we cannot, we do not, truly seek His glory by doing things our way. It must be His way. And His way is GRACE AND TRUTH.